Allotments

Also by Laurie Duggan

Poetry

East: Poems 1970–74 (1976)
Under the Weather (1978)
Adventures in Paradise (1982, 1991)
The Great Divide, Poems 1973–83 (1985)
The Ash Range (1987; 2nd edition, 2005*)
The Epigrams of Martial (1989)
Blue Notes (1990)
The Home Paddock (1991)
Memorials (1996)
New and Selected Poems, 1971–1993 (1996)
Mangroves (2003)
Compared to What: Selected Poems 1971–2003 (2005)*
The Passenger (2006)
Crab & Winkle (2009)*
The Epigrams of Martial (2010)
The Pursuit of Happiness (2012)*

Cultural history

Ghost Nation (2001)

*Shearsman titles

Laurie Duggan

Allotments

Shearsman Books

First published in the United Kingdom in 2014 by
Shearsman Books
50 Westons Hill Drive
Emersons Green
BRISTOL
BS16 7DF

Shearsman Books Ltd Registered Office
30–31 St. James Place, Mangotsfield, Bristol BS16 9JB
(this address not for correspondence)

www.shearsman.com

ISBN 978-1-84861-355-3

ACKNOWLEDGEMENTS
The first twenty-nine of these poems appeared as *Allotments* from
Jess Mynes' Fewer & Further Press in 2011 – a lovely small edition for
which Basil King provided the cover drawing. Allotments #66 and #67
appeared in draft form in the book of Vera Möller's King's Wood project
Fictional Hybrids (Stour Valley Arts, 2011). Allotment #2 appeared in
Eyewear (UK) as 'At the Norfolk Arms'. Other poems in the series have
appeared in *Black Box Manifold* (UK), *ETZ* (Australia) *Island* (Australia),
Mascara (Australia), *Steamer* (Germany/Australia), *The Harvard Review*
(USA), *The Recluse* (Poetry Project, USA), *this corner* (UK).
My thanks to all of the editors.

Allotments

Allotment #1

Live, at the local…
                              not, I imagine
like the bar in Rome Ken went to,
just one brooding Irish accent over by the log fire
the crunch of crisps… mine

women sing in the back bar,
the Irish guy and his son (?) are monosyllabic,
maybe a death in the family?
                                              though not a wake

I'm awake
                    not Paul Blackburn
                                                  the hops
dangle, as hops do
                              from the dark wood
(not the 'dark wood')
                                        the light gone by four
a gent reads the *Daily Telegraph*
                                              ('the darkness
surrounds us')
                              then orders a pint
without speaking a word

                              an old door
leads through to a French delicatessen,
bolted, probably, for decades

Allotment #2

At the Norfolk Arms
pressed tin and Corinthian columns
smoked *jamón* and cut glass,

a gilt Madonna hemmed
by dried peppers: W1 *español*.

This neighbourhood's Georgian,
the pub, named for Norfolk who?

Thomas Howard, the 4th duke,
Norfolk in Sussex, recusant?

The Spanish barman says
of the wine list I stare at
'the most expensive is the best'

I remember instead the edict
on an album cover
(*The Dictators Go Girl Crazy*):
'quantity *is* quality'

Allotment #3

halfway round the world
friends assemble an exhibition
of our former lives:
Coalcliff circa 1980;
photos of us, younger,
me washing dishes before the louvres,
out of my depth in a 'career move'
that didn't come off: scriptwriter
with skills for neither plot nor dialogue;
a house on sinking land,
(warped corner of the living room)

Allotment #4

William IV, Shoreditch
                    will anyone be here?

I have books to sell (ha ha)
                    and pints to go before I weep

I have at least figured out what to read
(give or take)

                    and, is it,
                    Apache?

                              not the Shadows:
a new version, ornate
with percussion, brass, organ and bells.

                    no sign of the poets…
                    or the audience
                    they're all, I suspect
                    at Allen Fisher's lecture

the sardines are good, with new potatoes, green beans and capers

                    scales fall from my teeth
                    if not my eyes

sufficient is the funk unto the day

                    still nobody here

though the guest beer
stands me well (if that
be the expression

                                        in, on, or about
                                        the promises

                        premises

strange rhyming voices
and clinked glass, a party
on the opposite table

                                the one-eyed
                                spill fewer beers

and the bust of (Beethoven?) blinded in one eye
on the upright,
a candle, stuffed birds,

                                                        art,
                                a blurry Rowlandson?

still no poets

                                                the music
                                                ramps up
I'm sonically enabled

                        13 ways
                        to stuff a blackbird

I'll be pissed off
if not pissed

                        a plucked guitar
and a 'sincere' piece of 'spoken word'

                        (Solomon Burke would do this better

'I'm so glad to be here tonight,
so glad to be in your wonderful city…'

                              (Everybody needs
                              somebody
                              to love their poems)

In advance of the broken arm
(the Broken Arms Hotel)

                                        Simon arrives.

there are now four people
(plus the poets)
                              an audience

Fat Billy on the wall

                    (William IV)

Allotment #5

Last days of the Gulbenkian? Possibly to be closed (or privatised)
& the last day of Olson (the reading group)

Koch warns about getting too universal
at the end of a long poem

                                     (his alter ego
(Olson's) fucks Gloucester harbour

                                        which gives birth to…?

except O is 'conventual' (as in a convent?)

then he mixes up his Greek gods
('But we *are* the Greeks'
        (Olson to Michael Anania))

                                  It was, I guess, easier
than scouring logbooks and citizens' accounts
                                      (O now famous
after Donald Allen, after the conferences

the gods wore suits
(or worked for the government)

                                    such the fate
                                    of epic
the breath of a man
struggling for same
                             in the light of lecture rooms

                                        my writing
cuts corners, loses
the thread

the notebook
steers towards November

towards (including) disorder

(Olson's final line: he'd lost the lot)

Allotment #6

Breakfast at Samphire
on the corner opposite, the Duke of Cumberland,
Knot's Yard

a friend across the road
too far away to signal
heads uphill for Whitstable station

small fluffy clouds
a promise of rain

                    will I walk the Crab & Winkle Way?
or bus it to Canterbury?

Allotment #7

for once, perfect clarity
the air heavy with malt
from Shepherd Neame

Allotment #8

a beer
in The Bear
where I've not been before

pressed tin
between the beams

a day barely exceeding 8 degrees

front doors
of The Sun

closed to the street, renovators
still at work

this narrow place (The Bear)
facing the guild Hall, the market square

fires not yet lit

I'll return to mine

Allotment #9

the small gnats
have ceased to wail;

dogwood's leaves lost
red branches bared

Allotment #10

The Sun half-full of builders
ceilings repainted
the back bar sheeted off with plastic

there are few people about
while this goes on

the fire stoked
the floor swept
the tools stowed

Allotment #11

November first 2010
Susan Howe
The Europe of Trusts

whose language?
Olson's?

                          a ghosted building
                          partly overgrown

a façade
the ribs behind

                   there are people in here
crowded before five p.m.

                       the book is on the table

earlier:
        rescued voices from old tapes
                           myself
aged five, 1954
              of that generation
who missed blitz and Atlantic sinkings but preceded the age
of universal terror (apart, that is, from The Bomb, though this
seems now an abstract concept, unlike the human version, the
small scale of a bus, a plane, a railway carriage
                     anyway, I was too young
to comprehend total annihilation

                   the crowd thins
at five o'clock

                    Howe's book on the table
(I've seen her sister read)

                    whose language?

Allotment #12

It was the golden age
of bad photocopying

a pound note,
grey and smudged,
half-size

            'little, all right'
            John Scannell said
to my comment 'it's a little beauty'

                    (this was, I think, 1966,
we had travelled to Festival Hall, Melbourne
for 'Battle of the Sounds'
(the year the Twilights won

                    (my school no longer exists

Allotment #13

                                        a man in a shapeless coat
enters and exits
a spectre
                        with vivid carry-bag

ghosted photographs

                                I was/wasn't here
                                now/then

the v-necked staff, maybe
didn't notice
                        I can't
position myself in history
so easily.

                        In 1967 I watched the world
on television. My mother borrowed
copies of the *San Francisco Oracle*
                                        In 1968

Music From Big Pink sounded
unlike anything I'd ever heard

Allotment #14

flower baskets
brave it out in London
before The Plough

a team of wheelchair users
cross the side street
accompanied by a couple
carrying ramps

I've forgotten my glasses
(meaning I can write
but not read

these marks
signify something

the dark closes in

who'll turn up tonight?
at the Swedenborg Centre

Allotment #15

draft and fire
(a window open in The Sun)

the till's shifted
to the bar

a new polished floor…

tiny insects hover round the taps

Allotment #16

in the wood stove
fire turns vaporous

a street
silent, Sunday afternoon

mulch around the hellebores
rudbeckias mostly beheaded

peripherally, a screen-saver glints

lavender hangs from the beams

a house
standing till now

its improbable history

what of the carpet's weave, of bore-holes in wood, slats
from the timbers of which ship, bound
for the Indies?

the flames

waver in sealed space

Allotment #17

again, waiting
(all lager, no ale)

light glimmer through drizzle
a gust from the east

someone reads *La Peste*
then talks of it in German

Cameron's Britain is
dark shapes beyond double-glazing

an imaginary space
where imagination is redundant

Allotment #18

Perseverance
(a title?)

en route to the Bus (Blue)
under a black sky

                                peruse a list (of books)
at a wobbly table

                        then down the road to Ciao Bella
for the one dish
I always have
            the poets
next door
in The Lamb

Allotment #19

soreness
of new shoes
on the train

a train through
nowhere

(an 'out of it' guy, slumped in the seat ahead)

into Essex
lights of motorways

RAINHAM STEEL
(the other Rainham)

evidence of life north of the Thames

Allotment #20

Uncommon

in the staff common room

next to a grand piano

(a baby grand)

a grand baby

amid microphones

a big (like Whalen)

...boobus

there was a lake outside

waterhens

a plinth on the lawn

unraked leaves

grey bricks, speckled with white stones

a roofline cut from the sky

remote

as pre-dynastic statuary

atomic

or adamic

the American Century

Allotment #21

slight airs on sea,
short waves,

the sound of talk from 1979
through rumble and tape hiss,

a conversation almost,
of import once,

distant voices consigned
to the unintelligible

Allotment #22

A new overpass at Canterbury West

smoky light

dried leaves above the butchers

a pile of carrots

Allotment #23

Sunlight, halo
on the Sheppey prison;

elsewhere, rain smudge,
backlit cloud

from Oare Marsh
to the Canterbury Downs

Allotment #24

laughter from the back bar
a party of architects

'it was all really crisp,
enormous pieces of glass'

scratches on a metal table,
accumulated stains, the image
upside down
of a pepper shaker

Allotment #25

'deep and crisp and even'
the snow

rudbeckias
brought down

finally (I thought)
spring back

with snow melt,
pinks too, as

trucks jacknife
on the motorways

Allotment #26

a frozen orange in the icebox
a disconnected battery
various items committed to memory sticks

Allotment #27

'I hate that colour,
it's like… curry'

eau de nil,
Nile water, or

oh, nihil
—this

the ceilings
(formerly red),

or olive (green)
a pale variety

Allotment #28

a dose of 'the finger' (Bishop's)
and the fire

someone else writes in this room, or types
on a notebook
                              a poem
a report (or both)

it's dead quiet on the street
where earlier in the day a Dutch truck
delivered flowers

a man with a black hat and cloak enters
(also with a folder)
                                        so the room has now three (3)
readers, writers, reporters

a season by the fire or
Un Saison d'Enfer

Allotment #29

snowdrop, then
daffodil, pink
on a rose branch, green
on a climber

suddenly parsley   then mint

Allotment #30

        knees to the bar
this man here: guess where he comes from?

it's busy tonight   nationality
in a world of fluid capital

                        Churchill's fingers suggest
'two more pints'

Allotment #31

arras over the banister
hides pots of conserve,

an old steam engine
roosts above the bread oven

someone talks strategy
the jargon of business school

ambulance lights on Station Road
'blue sky thinking' or 'stormy weather'

Allotment #32

                              a website
rumbles about commitment, what 'we' are to do
for Libya
                    write more poems?

(remember *Poetry of the Committed Individual*,
a title seeming at the time ludicrous, a vestige
of middle-class humanism

the front line is a household budget,
the immorality of bankers

Allotment #33

life in the margin:
spring, still winter-like

old men in trainers
walk on bunions

Allotment #34

back at The Sun
                        (beyond the…

I graph all this, with flattened accent
(drawn but not glottal)

(the test: 'This is Illyria, lady')

(I myself am a bracket,
a footnote
                        but this is as it should be

the smudge of a glass
set down on paper

this   this   this

Allotment #35

the impression of a bottle cut into a wall
above it a trophy (a crown or a hand,
hard to tell in the half-dark

Allotment #36

a morning frost, bent stems
then a clear sky,
ongoing chores

Allotment #37

shadows in the window
seeming people,
spaces between
a flame's reflection

nails not quite hammered in

a rattle of cutlery

the mechanics of a worn philosophy

my work irrelevant as
an immense puzzle, lifelong

Allotment #38

the Piccadilly line below,
footfalls on the floor above

this is the space of the poem

Allotment #39

Europe, out there somewhere
old cannon on a cliff
above the café

Allotment #40

radio at 4 a.m.
news of an earthquake, the second
in a month on the Pacific fault
as in 'whose'?
                          things happen
they're not punishment, we just
(Shintō) have to deal with them

Allotment #41

a robin lands, curious
as I grub weeds

Allotment #42

above the window a bellows
stone bottles (Morandi)
a kerosene lantern, old books

Lamb's Conduit,
March 15th

Allotment #43

birdsong in the dark:
ruddock, not nightingale

Allotment #44

I'm seated at 'my' table in the corner,
a view of the bar. Writing on the window reads:

THE SUN INN

FINEST ALES and PORTER

which is almost POETRY

      someone speaks in a Slavonic language:
      the words 'Casablanca' and 'Gestapo' audible

I keep thinking of John Forbes' line:
'spent tracer flecks Baghdad's night sky'
that I would hear as 'Spencer Tracy'

      this is a Humphrey Bogart occasion

these men, in camouflage,
leave the bar

Allotment #45

late afternoon light in Faversham

little England

'it's really not poetry

is it?'

Allotment #46

'about seven months I been locked up
and what good did that do me . . .'

(the daughter 'over in Sheppey',
the mother 'living in a tent')

'you ain't got nothing to offer me babe (spits)
you don't offer me shit!'

(she drinks more brandy)

the publican intervenes,
they apologise, resume

Allotment #47

peacock
brimstone &
gold tip

(a field note)

Allotment #48

a goldfinch in
the herb garden

Allotment #49

                          a moment's silence
with Gael Turnbull,
Brigflatts Meeting House, 1987

                                   later
on Hardknott Pass
November cold

(posted there
                 Legionaries
from Africa

Allotment #50

no rain south of the river

'groups from Manchester
will not be welcome'

Allotment #51

sudden foreclosures

the state of the nation

Allotment #52

Robert Duncan at
                    Bernie O'Regan's?
a hand
          measuring beats
                              insisting
community

some eight of us,
                    Melbourne, 1975
(my clothes testify)

    occult equals outside the purview
    of the Enlightenment.

          I'd sourced modernism
for convention
                    grew later
to love the madness of those
excised from history

Allotment #53

cygnets on the marsh

red fox in the forest

Allotment #54

war stories from the neighbour table

the fold of a year

a middle-aged man labelled 'Unknown Pleasures'

Allotment #55

                       to be absolutely modern,
not to compete with history

Miró suggests this much

burnt canvas
reveals the frame

Allotment #56

a wall of dog rose, ivy,
spiky pyrocanthus

from which the mechanic twitter
of blackbird chicks

Allotment #57

lift two small garden pots
strain a muscle

shoeleaces impossible to tie
you depend on rain

white shock
in lieu of transverse abdominals

the mind drained of sense

Allotment #58

fog at night
on the Wye Downs

the road 'insistent'
through the village

Allotment #59

stained floorboards, parallel
toward sunlight

at 6 p.m., a universe
out there

where to place
the chamomile?

Allotment #60

black edge of typeface
magnified, blurred

moving away each volume,
decades compressed

the poems, a view
of the street out there

a coffee vendor
the space of a window

Allotment #61

my head missed the beam
the back door of Monk's House
but scraped the gutter

I touched (illegally) Henry Green's
Pack My Bags (the books
not to be handled)

they would walk between houses
across the South Downs,

felt the cold less than us
though servants dug their cess pits

from rear of the vegetable patch
the land falls away to the Ouse

where she sank, Mrs Woolf,
weighted by stones

Allotment #62

to make much of little
where perception and act are one

each thing in its place
spread over the garden

poppy seeds of various hue
stolen from elsewhere

Allotment #63

heavy summer

(an English thing)

Allotment #64

the moon
red & gibbous
over Rochester

Allotment #65

sun on a curve of brick
blue monkshood
beneath a trellis

Allotment #66

coppiced beech
a dumped mattress

soft mould under dead yew leaves

    red wood ants build hills with these splinters
    some distance from the source

**WARNING // Do not play
on the sculptures**

    these have disappeared
    replaced by foxgloves

        an artist's name, a date, a serial number
        but no art

instead
a sachet of HP sauce on the track

Allotment #67

a threshold of sorts:
at the edge of a harvested field
a gap in the hedge, then
'the midst of a dark forest'

dusky fallow deer disperse
—the guttural bark of a doe

noon light penetrates these yews

fungus, yellow
on rotten wood

Allotment #68

some way from the sea
on a previous shoreline

The Ship (and all
who sail in her

a U-boat in an English canal
smelling of pub gravy

Allotment #69

those houses on Abbey Street opposite the Phoenix,
gutters hidden behind the façade

a single vertical strip of windows
(above the door a blank wall)

openings that suggest space
and height (a Georgian ceiling)

the whole view squared by the bar window
a shadow-play: figures intent for the pub

Allotment #70

a bust in the first floor window of the Guildhall
seemed a real person addressing the room

false clock faces on three walls of the tower
a fourth marks approximate time

the dragon on the roof faces south-west,
an Autumn wind from the Channel

Allotment #71

The front bar of the Bear,
quiet at this hour, a smell of Brasso

and a hint of rain, of more perhaps,
a speckled pigeon crosses the square

passing the headless dummy outside the Op Shop,
Carter's Newsagent closes,

the pitch of the roof above the stationers
almost mansard with lead ridges

everything grey and white (white
of buildings, grey of sky) and red brick

Allotment #72

plants hang from window boxes above the wine merchant
(boarded-up)

       the sweeper grins as he shovels trash

tattooed on a man's neck
outside the Lord Russell:

          LARRY
          14-02-11
          HONEY

then 'Telstar', Margaret Thatcher's favourite tune

a herald of free-enterprise?

a hint that the rich might, fifty years on,
escape this ruined planet?

Down Marchmont Street
           little flying saucers
glide along a sushi counter
all that is solid melts into air

Allotment #73

virginia creeper,
red on a far wall
under a rusted vent

Allotment #74

long grass, gnats
to shoulder height,

the North Sea:
distant, cerulean, a pink strand

far side of the mud flats,
the racket of migrating birds

Allotment #75

fruit machine flicker
far side of the bar

on a windy street
the ghost of a paper bag

Allotment #76

for days I did nothing
ninth floor (Philosophy)
of the Menzies Building

Colin stomped around my room
shouting lines from *The Sonnets*

       'It is 5:15 a.m.   Dear Marge, hello'

Allotment #77

carved on the surface of a
dresser, the mark of Zorro

(an early act of vandalism)

Allotment #78

yellow leaves on the Red Road

shaggy inkcap

Allotment #79

'standing water'

Allotment #80

moderate or good,
occasionally poor

Allotment #81

a phrase recurred
in the mouths of friends,

1972, hallucinating
in backyard Sydney

a radio voice
from the thirties:

all over Europe
the lights are going out

Allotment #82

knobs of black fungus,
Cramp Balls or
King Alfred's Cakes,

white saucers (brackets)
off the stump

Allotment #83

small poodle
in the barmaid's arms

extractor fan
stuffed with newsprint

old music above the Stour
as the miller told his tale

Allotment #84

'beware the moon
and stick to the road'
(advice for drunks)
above the bar of The Dolphin

the clientele post-prandial at 3 pm
as the light fails, in a street
named for St Radigund, poet,
friend to Gregory of Tours

Greek patterns on frosted glass,
the pargeted wall opposite
all scallop and rectangle
above a low green door

Allotment #85

lights upside-down on water

a Soviet sub marooned on the Medway

Allotment #86

gypsophila, a threat
of hail in late Spring

Allotment #87

a hare approaching,
ears upright, at first
an unlikely rabbit

Allotment #88

green suddenly
on branches

beyond the wall,
in half-light, faint

movement of leaf
before gable

is it wisteria (?)
that mauve, crossed

by wires two
backyards up

gulls cut across
a sky, now cloudless

a round stone balanced
on a brick

Allotment #89

a glass box
over a swamp

cut off from Northfleet
and Swanscombe

by truck routes, undergrowth,
an artificial hill

churches precarious
above chalk cuttings

Allotment #90

lighters, erased signage
of ex-wharves

Allotment #91

wind sock on the lawn
behind the manor

the plateau tails off
into stubble,

a wood, a dip
to a dry valley

a steep climb past a stile
to a church

far enough from anywhere
to be left open

Allotment #92

Margate, an approaching storm, 11.40am
red lights reflected from the esplanade

distant sun on tankers & wind farms
North Sea salt on the glass

Allotment #93

All Hallows approaches
the bar strung with rubber bats,

telescopes, astrolabes
obscure the windows.

Pepys drank in this pub
(the Thames, Wapping

above the tunnel
to Rotherhithe)

further out, rotten wharves,
hulks on the estuary bed

empty sea-forts
subject to slow rust

Allotment #94

October sun
two pink leaves above the sill

diagonal panes on carpet
fade and reappear

Allotment #95

white buildings
over the old town

a park bench, empty
on the slope

suitable enough
for pathos

a Bob Dickerson figure:
green man

head bent,
oblivious humans

dog-walk
on the horizon

Allotment #96

high pitch of a robin

the last dogwood leaves

damp soil for months

Allotment #97

the house white,
it's Moroccan (or Mauretanian,
how would I know),
the music's almost dub

knotted tiles,
endless inscriptions
edge towards: John James
Live at Free Range,
one night in November 2013

art paper?   or Art Pepper?

the hour approaches

Allotment #98

'Les Dawson is so fucking brilliant'

       a man shifts a rucksack across the floor
             drinks a short black

this is 'osterria terranostra'
        Sicilian and Sardinian regional cuisine

a potted plant traverses the room
another appears from below stairs

garlic cloves frame a mirror
next to a room labelled 'masculi'

           the underworld on Farringdon Road

that strange shape on a rack
       reveals itself as a smoked ham

below it, a flag features a woman's face
       transposed onto three legs

'I've sung in the Royal Albert Hall
and again that's a different sound you get.
It depends upon your hearing and everything else...'

Allotment #99

a red irruption
about the right eye

weakness in the calves

expected floods

                    then Paul Klee

        his inscriptions

(!!!!!!!!)

                outside the gallery:

floodlight

                    a rumble
                    under the Thames

Allotment #100

a circle of stage lights
point at nothing in particular
luxuriating pink sofas
                              cold air
seeps through some crack in space

last night's chill
en route to the Anchor

this morning a broken tile replaced
hinges of a door straightened

Lightning Source UK Ltd.
Milton Keynes UK
UKOW03f1322280414

230709UK00001B/6/P